S0-AFQ-108

Marie-Victoire Garcia

marinades

Photographs by Akiko Ida
Styling by Laura Zavan

contents

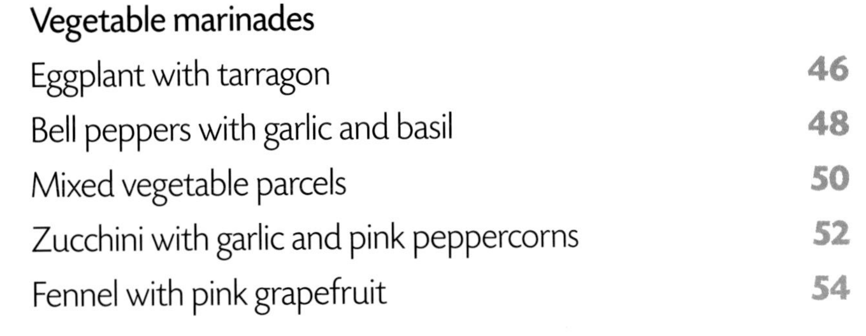

Vegetable marinades

Fruit marinades

Tricks of the trade

A pleasure for the palate

The very word 'marinade' conjures up the image and taste of spices and mixed herbs used to prepare meat, fish, vegetables and fruit with a wide range of different flavors.

Marinades are a pleasure for the palate and offer endless opportunities for discovering new flavors and aromas.

Quick and easy to prepare

Whether cooked or uncooked, marinades are easy to prepare.

All you need do is make a seasoning of herbs and spices with oil or sauces, mix it with meat, fish, vegetables or fruit, and leave to marinate in the refrigerator for anything from a few minutes to a few hours, or even overnight.

The main part of the process, a sort of pre-cooking, takes care of itself.

Give it time to do its work and let the flavor of the herbs and spices in the marinade permeate the raw ingredients.

Soy sauce is a popular marinade ingredient and is easily obtainable in supermarkets, but it is important to choose the right one. *Light* soy sauce is light in color, full of flavor and the best choice for cooking, while *dark* soy sauce is richer, better for stews, and also makes an excellent dipping sauce.

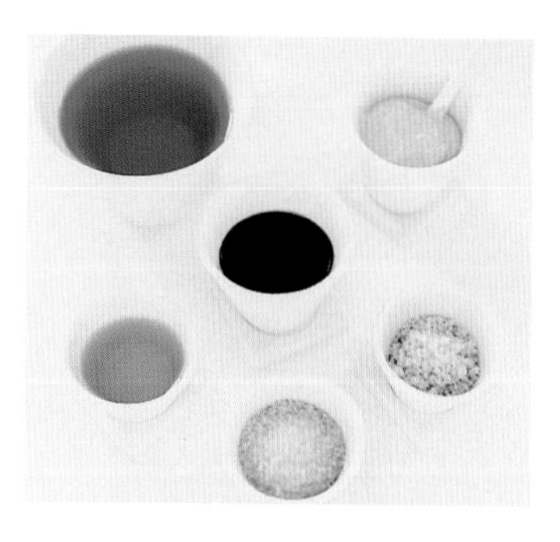

Uncooked marinades

Uncooked marinades consist of an oil- or lemon-based seasoning that permeates the food—the length of marinating time depends on the type of food.

Not only does the food assimilate the flavor of the herbs or spices, it is also 'cooked' by the lemon juice or vinegar used in the marinade.

Food prepared and flavored in this way can be eaten raw. It therefore goes without saying that meat and fish must be ultra-fresh.

Some vegetables, such as bell peppers, can be cooked before being marinated. This makes them a little more digestible.

Cooked marinades

Generally speaking, meat and certain types of fish are better prepared in a cooked marinade.

Marinating is a form of aromatic "pre-cooking" that tenderizes the flesh and gives it more flavour.

The oil used in the marinade prevents the meat or fish from drying out during cooking, whether it is broiled, pan fried, roasted, or baked in the oven.

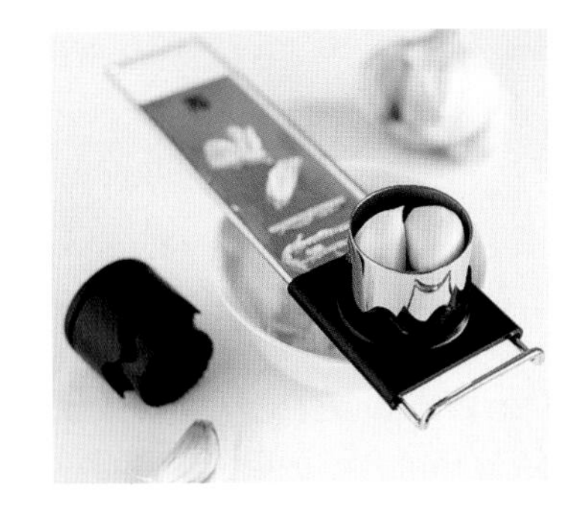

The right tools

Because the food has marinated in a seasoning containing oil, there's no need to add more oil when cooking. However, you would be well advised to use a nonstick skillet, especially for dishes using sugar or honey. These two ingredients have a tendency to stick to the bottom of even a slightly worn pan during cooking.

Garlic is often used in marinades, except fruit marinades, of course. The ideal tool for dealing with garlic cloves is a garlic grater but a garlic press works just as well.

Sliced chicken with cinnamon

Pour 4 personnes

1 handful raisins

1 lb skinless chicken breasts, sliced thinly

3 tablespoons olive oil

1½ tablespoons cinnamon

1 teaspoon Demerara sugar

3½ tablespoons water

marinade

5 tablespoons light soy sauce

Soak the raisins in a bowl of boiling water.

Place the sliced chicken in a shallow dish, add the soy sauce and turn the slices so that they are well coated with the sauce. Cover with plastic wrap and leave to marinate in the refrigerator for 30 minutes.

Heat the olive oil in a skillet and fry the chicken over high heat, turning constantly. Sprinkle with the cinnamon and brown sugar and stir well. Add the measured water, cover, and leave to simmer over low heat for about 15 minutes.

Drain the raisins and add to the pan. Mix well and leave to simmer over low heat for 5 minutes. Serve immediately.

Serving suggestion

Couscous makes an ideal accompaniment for this sweet-and-sour dish.

Chicken escalopes with mint

Serves 4

4 chicken escalopes, cut from the breast

a few fresh mint leaves

marinade

juice of 2 limes

juice of 1 lemon

4 tablespoons light soy sauce

4 tablespoons red wine

3 tablespoons olive oil

6–7 sprigs fresh mint, finely chopped

2 garlic cloves, peeled and chopped

Put all the ingredients for the marinade into a shallow dish and mix well.

Cut the chicken escalopes in half and add to the marinade. Mix well to coat and then cover with plastic wrap and leave to marinate in the refrigerator for 1 hour.

Heat a cast-iron griddle pan or nonstick skillet and cook the escalopes for 5–7 minutes on each side. As the chicken begins to dry out, moisten with the marinade. Sprinkle with a few mint leaves and serve immediately.

Serving suggestion

In early summer a salad of tomato, cucumber and scallions or salad onions, seasoned with white wine vinegar and a pinch of sugar, makes an ideal accompaniment for this dish.

Chicken breasts with honey

Serves 4

2 large chicken breasts

marinade

3 tablespoons white wine vinegar

2 tablespoons Worcestershire sauce

2 tablespoons clear honey

1 tablespoon olive oil

1 garlic clove, peeled and crushed

¼ teaspoon fresh oregano

pinch of fresh thyme

freshly ground black pepper

Remove the skin from the chicken breasts, cut them in half and place in a shallow dish. Mix together all the ingredients for the marinade, pour over the chicken breasts and turn to coat well. Cover with plastic wrap and leave to marinate in the refrigerator for 1 hour.

Preheat the grill on a high setting, if it is above the oven, or at an oven setting of 400°F if the grill is in the roof of the oven.

Arrange the chicken breasts in an ovenproof dish and place under the preheated broiler. Cook for 5 minutes and then turn the broiler down to a medium setting or reduce the oven temperature to 350°F. Turn the chicken breasts and broil for 5–10 minutes on each side, depending on their thickness.

Tandoori chicken legs

Serves 4

4 chicken legs (drumstick and thigh)

juice of 1 lemon

2 tablespoons olive oil

salt

1 tablespoon cilantro leaves

4 lemon slices

marinade

1½ cups plain yogurt

2 tablespoons white wine vinegar

2 tablespoons olive oil

2 tablespoons Tandoori spice mixture (available from Indian stores, or some supermarkets)

The day before you want to serve this dish, remove the skin from the chicken legs and deeply score the flesh. Sprinkle with lemon juice, season with salt and arrange the chicken in an ovenproof dish.

Mix together all the ingredients for the marinade and pour over the chicken. Cover with plastic wrap and leave to marinate overnight in the refrigerator.

The next day, drizzle each leg with olive oil and cook in a preheated oven at 350°F for 45 minutes. Sprinkle with fresh cilantro leaves and serve immediately with lemon slices.

Serving suggestion

Serve with a bowl of diced cucumber mixed with plain yogurt, olive oil, crushed garlic, salt, and chopped mint. You can also serve with Basmati rice for a more substantial meal.

Sesame chicken

Serves 4

2 chicken breasts

1 teaspoon sesame seeds

marinade

3 tablespoons dark soy sauce

juice of 1 lemon

1 tablespoon clear honey

1 tablespoon sesame oil

2 garlic cloves, peeled and sliced

½ teaspoon crushed hot chile pepper

1 teaspoon ground cumin

freshly ground black pepper

Remove the skin from the chicken breasts and cut lengthwise into 1 inch pieces. Place in a shallow dish. Mix together all the ingredients for the marinade and pour over the chicken pieces. Cover with plastic wrap and leave to marinate in the refrigerator for 1 hour.

Heat a nonstick skillet over high heat and brown the chicken pieces, stirring constantly and adding the marinade at regular intervals until the pieces are slightly caramelized.

Turn the chicken into a serving dish and sprinkle with the sesame seeds.

Serving suggestion

Rice makes an ideal accompaniment for this delicious sesame-flavored dish.

Citrus chicken drumsticks

Serves 4

8 chicken drumsticks

olive oil

marinade

juice of 2 oranges

juice of 1 lemon

1 teaspoon olive oil

1 garlic clove, peeled and finely chopped

1 teaspoon each chopped fresh rosemary, thyme and oregano

salt and freshly ground black pepper

Remove the skin from the chicken drumsticks, score the flesh and arrange the drumsticks in a shallow dish. (The skin can be kept on if preferred.)

Mix together all the ingredients for the marinade and pour over the chicken. Cover with plastic wrap and leave to marinate in the refrigerator for 30 minutes.

Preheat the oven to 400°F.

Brush the drumsticks with olive oil, place in an ovenproof dish and pour over the marinade. Cook in the oven for 20 minutes, spooning the marinade over the chicken at regular intervals. Check that the drumsticks are cooked by piercing with a sharp skewer to make sure the juices run clear.

Serving suggestion

A salad of fennel, onions, olives, and orange segments, seasoned with olive oil and the juice of half an orange, will bring out the flavor of this dish.

Variation

If you like onions, add a finely chopped scallion to the marinade.

Chicken kabobs with rosemary and basil

Serves 4

4 skinless boned chicken breasts

2 tablespoons olive oil

marinade

juice of 3 lemons

1 tablespoon olive oil

1 garlic clove, peeled and crushed

2 tablespoons fresh rosemary

1 tablespoon fresh basil

½ teaspoon freshly ground black pepper

8 wooden skewers

Cut the chicken breasts into 1¼-inch pieces.

Mix together all the ingredients for the marinade in a shallow dish, add the chicken pieces and mix well. Cover with plastic wrap and leave to marinate in the refrigerator for 2 hours.

Soak the skewers in warm water to prevent them burning during cooking. Thread the chicken pieces onto the skewers.

Heat the olive oil in a nonstick skillet and add the kabobs, turning so that they brown on all sides and gradually brushing with the rest of the marinade while they are cooking.

Serving suggestion

A tomato salad seasoned with olive oil will bring out the flavor of the basil, while a salad of orange segments will emphasize the rosemary.

Asian-style beef tenderloin

Serves 4

piece of beef tenderloin, about 1 lb

1 leek

8 oz fresh spinach leaves

2 tablespoons olive, or grapeseed, oil

marinade

1 small bunch flat-leaf parsley

2 garlic cloves, peeled

2 tablespoons light soy sauce

2 tablespoons oyster sauce

2 tablespoons olive oil

1 teaspoon sugar

4 tablespoons water

This dish is best prepared using a wok but if you don't have one, a nonstick skillet will do.

To prepare the marinade, finely chop the parsley and garlic. Mix together with the soy sauce, oyster sauce, olive oil, and sugar. Stir thoroughly and pour the marinade into a dish.

Cut the beef (in the direction of the fibers) into thin strips about 1 1/4–1 1/2 inches long and add to the marinade. Mix well, cover the dish with plastic wrap, and leave to marinate in the refrigerator for at least 4 hours.

Trim and clean the leek and cut into strips about 1 1/4–1 1/2 inches long by 1/2 inch wide. Rinse the spinach leaves, remove any thick stalks, and cut the leaves in half if they are on the big side.

Remove the strips of beef from the marinade, add the measured water and stir well.

Heat 1 tablespoon of the oil in a wok, or skillet, over high heat. When the oil is hot (it will start smoking), add the beef and stir continuously for 1–2 minutes, depending on how well done you like your meat. Remove the beef and keep to one side.

Heat the remaining oil in the wok and fry the leek for 1 minute over high heat, stirring constantly. Pour on the marinade, add the beef, followed by the spinach. Cover and cook for 1 minute over low heat.

Serving suggestion

Flavored rice makes an ideal accompaniment for this Asian-style beef dish.

Beef tenderloin with garlic and ginger

Serves 4

piece of beef tenderloin, about 1 lb

1 tablespoon olive, or grapeseed, oil

marinade

3 tablespoons light soy sauce

5 tablespoons sherry vinegar

2 garlic cloves, peeled and chopped

1 piece fresh ginger (3/4 inch), peeled and minced

freshly ground black pepper

Preheat the oven to 425°F.

Heat the oil in a flameproof casserole or cooking pot, over high heat. Fry the beef for 5 minutes, turning from time to time to make sure it is browned on all sides.

Place the casserole into the oven and cook the beef for 15 minutes, or longer if you like your meat well done.

While the meat is cooking, prepare the marinade by mixing together all the ingredients in a shallow dish. There's no need to add salt—the soy sauce is salty enough.

Remove the beef from the oven and leave to cool. Slice thinly and add to the marinade. Cover with plastic wrap and leave to marinate in the refrigerator for 1 hour, turning the slices at regular intervals.

Just before serving, remove the beef from the marinade—this can be served in a separate bowl for guests who like to dip their meat in the sauce.

Serving suggestion

The marinated beef goes equally well with warm rice or raw vegetables, for example cucumber, carrot, zucchini, and celery batons.

Pork chops with honey and cardamom

Serves 4

8 pork chops

marinade

2 tablespoons clear honey

2 tablespoons olive oil

2 garlic cloves, peeled and chopped

½ teaspoon ground cardamom seeds (see handy hint below)

½ teaspoon fresh thyme

salt and freshly ground black pepper

Mix together all the ingredients for the marinade. Lay the chops in a large shallow dish and pour over the marinade, turning the chops to coat well. Cover with plastic wrap and leave to marinate in the refrigerator for 1 hour.

Heat a nonstick skillet over high heat and add the pork chops. When they are nicely browned on both sides, reduce the heat and cook for a further 10 minutes, turning from time to time. If the chops begin to stick during cooking, add a little water. As there are 8 chops, you may need to fry them in two batches —keep the first batch warm while cooking the second.

Serving suggestion

Serve with sliced cucumber for a "light bite," or with rice and dark soy sauce (for dipping) for a more exotic meal (see Quick and easy to prepare on page 4.)

You can make a simple, tasty dip by mixing 3 tablespoons tomato ketchup and 1 tablespoon Worcestershire sauce with a few drops of Tabasco.

Handy hint

Cardamom seeds are sold loose or ground but it's best to buy the seeds (or in pods) and grind them yourself, as ground cardamom quickly loses its flavor.

Lamb kabobs with cumin and coriander

Serves 4

500 g/1 lb boned shoulder of lamb (or thick slices cut from the top of the leg)

1 tablespoon olive oil

marinade

1 onion, peeled and chopped

1 garlic clove, peeled and crushed

juice of 1 lemon

3 tablespoons olive oil

1 teaspoon ground cumin

1 teaspoon ground coriander

½ teaspoon ground ginger

salt and freshly ground black pepper

8 wooden skewers

Mix together all the ingredients for the marinade in a shallow dish. Cut the lamb into several pieces and add to the marinade. Mix well, turning the pieces to coat. Cover with plastic wrap and leave to marinate in the refrigerator overnight.

Soak the skewers in warm water so that they don't burn during cooking. Cut the lamb into cubes and thread them onto the skewers.

Heat the olive oil in a nonstick skillet, over moderate heat, and cook the kabobs, turning frequently. You may prefer to broil them. Lamb is best served not too well done.

Serving suggestion

Sliced zucchini, sautéed in a skillet for 10–15 minutes and sprinkled with chopped cilantro just before serving, make an ideal accompaniment for the kabobs.

Veal escalopes with orange

Serves 4

4 veal escalopes

1 unwaxed, or well-scrubbed, orange

marinade

juice of two oranges

juice of 1 lemon

1 teaspoon brown Demerara sugar

2 tablespoons olive oil

1 bunch fresh thyme, chopped

salt and freshly ground black pepper

Place the escalopes in a shallow dish. Mix together all the ingredients for the marinade and pour over the veal, turning to coat well. Cover with plastic wrap and leave to marinate in the refrigerator for 3 hours, turning the meat from time to time.

Carefully pare the rind from the orange with a zester or vegetable knife, avoiding any pith.

Heat a cast-iron griddle or nonstick skillet over moderate heat and cook the escalopes for 5–7 minutes on each side, depending on their thickness. Moisten from time to time with the marinade.

Serve immediately sprinkled with the orange rind.

Serving suggestion

Sliced zucchini browned in olive oil and garlic really bring out the flavor of this dish.

Duckling breasts with pink peppercorns and coriander

Serves 4

2 duckling breasts

1 teaspoon black peppercorns

1 tablespoon pink peppercorns, whole

1 teaspoon pink peppercorns, crushed

4–6 coriander seeds, crushed

1 head red (Treviso) endive

marinade

1 tablespoon balsamic vinegar

juice of 1 orange

1 tablespoon mild mustard

2 tablespoons clear honey

2 tablespoons grapeseed or groundnut oil

2 tablespoons walnut oil

salt

The day before you are serving the dish, remove the skin and fat from the duckling breasts and place them in a shallow dish. Sprinkle with black peppercorns, whole and crushed pink peppercorns and coriander seeds. Cover with plastic wrap and leave to marinate in the refrigerator overnight.

The following day, mix together all the ingredients for the marinade. Cut the breasts into thin strips, place them in a dish and pour over three-quarters of the marinade. Cover with plastic wrap and marinate in the refrigerator for 1 hour.

Rinse the chicory leaves and dry with a salad spinner or on paper towels. Arrange on individual plates and season with the rest of the marinade. Place the strips of duckling carefully on the bed of endive.

Serving suggestion

A few croutons added to each plate will give the dish extra “crunch.”

Shrimp in citrus juice

Serves 4

1 unwaxed, or well-scrubbed, orange

1¾ lb cooked shrimp, unpeeled

olive oil

marinade

juice of 1 orange

juice of ½ lemon

2 tablespoons olive oil

1 garlic clove, peeled and crushed

6–7 sprigs flat-leaf parsley, finely chopped

salt and freshly ground black pepper

Wash the orange, blot dry with paper towels and grate half the rind, or remove in thin strips with a zester.

Peel the shrimp without removing their tails and place in a shallow dish.

Mix together all the ingredients for the marinade and pour over the shrimp. Mix well, turning the prawns to coat, cover with plastic wrap and leave to marinate in the refrigerator for about 1 hour.

Divide the shrimp between individual dishes, drizzle with olive oil, and scatter over the grated orange rind or strips of zest. Serve immediately.

Variation

To give this entrée a slightly exotic flavor, add a few pinches of curry powder to the marinade and replace the parsley with chopped cilantro.

Sardines with mixed herbs

Serves 4

12 sardines

crusty loaf

marinade

1 bunch each fresh chives, dill, and chervil

1 teaspoon dried oregano (optional)

juice of 3 lemons

3/4 cup olive oil

6 scallions, peeled and very thinly sliced

salt and freshly ground black pepper

Rinse the fresh herbs and blot dry with paper towels. Chop and mix well, adding the dried oregano if using.

Slit the underside of the sardines (taking care not to cut through the back), then gut them and remove the backbone (see Handy hint below). Cut off the tails and any overhanging skin on the sides, wash carefully and blot dry with paper towels. Place the open sardines, skin side down, in a dish.

Drizzle with the lemon juice and then the olive oil. Top with the sliced scallions, season with salt and pepper, and sprinkle evenly with three-quarters of the mixed herbs. Shake the dish so that the sardines are well coated with the marinade, cover with plastic wrap, and leave to marinate in the refrigerator for 2 hours.

Serving suggestion

Serve the sardines on slices of toasted crusty bread, topped with a few scallion rings, and the remaining herbs.

You can also accompany the sardines with a cherry tomato salad seasoned with olive oil and topped with a few scallion rings and mixed herbs.

Handy hint

To remove the backbone: after slitting the underside and gutting the sardine, open it out, place cut side down on the work surface and press along the backbone with your thumbs. Turn the fish over and pull the backbone out.

Tuna with ginger

Serves 4

4 slices fresh tuna

marinade

seeds from 1 tablespoon cardamon pods

juice of 3 limes

3 tablespoons olive oil

1 onion, peeled and chopped

2 garlic cloves, peeled and crushed

piece fresh ginger (3/4 inch), peeled and grated

Crush the cardamon pods in a mortar and remove all the small brown-black seeds (see handy hint on page 24.)

Place the tuna slices in a shallow dish.

Mix together all the ingredients for the marinade and pour over the tuna, making sure the slices are well coated. Cover the dish with plastic wrap and leave to marinate in the refrigerator for 2 hours.

Heat a cast-iron griddle or nonstick skillet and cook the tuna slices on high heat, for 2–3 minutes, turning and moistening with the marinade as soon as the fish begins to dry out. Serve immediately.

Serving suggestion

Cold rice noodles seasoned with sesame oil make an ideal accompaniment for this dish.

Fillets of fresh cod with cilantro and fennel

Serves 4

1 lb fresh cod fillets

small bunch cilantro, finely chopped

marinade

juice of 3 lemons

5 tablespoons olive oil

1/4 teaspoon fennel seeds

1/4 teaspoon cumin seeds

pinch Cayenne pepper

salt

Mix together all the ingredients for the marinade.

Slice the cod fillets into thin strips and arrange in a shallow dish.

Pour the marinade over the fillets, turning to coat, cover with plastic wrap and leave to marinate in the refrigerator for at least 2 hours.

Just before serving, sprinkle with the chopped cilantro.

Variation

You can replace the cod with another fish—sea bream or bass will work just as well.

Anglerfish with lime and cilantro

Serves 4

1 lb anglerfish fillets

1 red salad onion

½ red chile, seeds removed

6 small, firm tomatoes

3 tablespoons olive oil

30 cilantro leaves (20 chopped, 10 left whole)

salt

marinade

juice of 2 limes

Cut the fish fillets into long, thin slices, about 1¼ inches thick, and place in a shallow dish. Pour over the lime juice and turn the fish to make sure it is well coated. Cover with plastic wrap and leave to marinate in the refrigerator for 1 hour.

Peel and thinly slice the onion. Rinse and cut the chile into small dice. Rinse and thinly slice the tomatoes, removing the seeds. Put the vegetables in a shallow dish, drizzle with olive oil, season with salt, and scatter with the chopped cilantro leaves.

Remove the fish from the refrigerator, drain and arrange on individual plates. Top with the mixed vegetables and sprinkle with a few whole cilantro leaves.

Serving suggestion

Slices of avocado double as an ideal accompaniment and garnish for this dish.

Salmon marinated in curry sauce

Serves 4

1 salmon fillet, about 1¼ lb

1 avocado

marinade (overnight)

4 tablespoons coarse sea salt

2 tablespoons sugar

freshly ground black pepper

marinade (on the day)

juice of 1 unwaxed lemon, and the rind pared into thin strips with a zester

1 level tablespoon curry powder

½ bunch fresh chives, finely chopped

1 small red chile, seeds removed

1 sprig fresh dill or fennel, finely chopped

¾ cup olive oil

2 red bell peppers

1 tomato, diced

salt

freshly ground black pepper

The day before you want to serve the dish, place the salmon fillet in a shallow dish and sprinkle with the coarse sea salt, sugar and black pepper. Cover with plastic wrap and chill in the refrigerator overnight.

Cut the bell peppers into quarters, remove the seeds, and place under a preheated broiler, skin side up, for 20 minutes (see recipe on page 48). Remove the peppers from the broiler and wrap in a plastic bag for 30 minutes to loosen the skins. Peel and cut the flesh into thin strips and place in a salad bowl. Cover with plastic wrap and chill in the refrigerator overnight.

The following day, mix together the lemon juice and rind, curry powder, chopped chives, chile, chopped dill (or fennel), and olive oil. Season with salt and pepper. Remove the peppers from the refrigerator and add the diced tomato. Pour over the marinade and mix well.

Remove the salmon from the refrigerator, rinse in cold water, and blot dry with paper towels. Cut into cubes, add to the vegetable marinade, mix in well, and return to the refrigerator for at least 2 hours.

At the last minute, peel and cube the avocado and serve with the salmon (don't prepare until just before serving as it may discolor). Serve well chilled.

Scallops with Cointreau

Serves 4

1 lb scallops, fresh (without the coral) or frozen

rind of 1 orange

1 teaspoon brown Demerara sugar

4 tablespoons/½ stick butter

scant ½ cup Cointreau

¾ cup crème fraîche or creamy plain yogurt (not low fat or it will separate while cooking)

marinade

¾ cup Cointreau

Defrost frozen scallops. Rinse the fresh or defrosted scallops and pat dry with paper towels. If the scallops are large, cut into small pieces, and place in a shallow dish. Pour over the ¾ cup Cointreau and mix well to coat. Cover with plastic wrap and leave to marinate in the refrigerator for 2 hours.

Cut the orange rind into thin strips, remove the white pith and drop the strips of rind into a small pan of boiling water. Add the brown sugar and stir well. Leave to boil for 5 minutes and then strain the rind.

Remove the scallops from the refrigerator and discard the marinade. Melt the butter in a skillet, over a medium heat, and lightly fry the scallops for 5 minutes. Pour on the scant ½ cup Cointreau and flambé.

Add the crème fraîche, or yogurt, to the pan, mix well, then reduce the sauce over high heat for 5 minutes.

Divide the scallops between individual plates, cover with the sauce and sprinkle with orange peel.

Serving suggestion

White rice mixed with wild rice makes an attractive and tasty accompaniment.

Eggplant with tarragon

Serves 4

6 small eggplants

marinade

1 tablespoon balsamic vinegar

5 tablespoons olive oil

4 garlic cloves, crushed

2–3 tarragon sprigs, leaves stripped

salt and freshly ground black pepper

This dish can be prepared a day in advance. If you do, the eggplant will absorb more of the tarragon flavor.

Rinse the eggplants, cut each into 4 lengthwise and then into 1-inch pieces. Cook in a steamer for 15 minutes (start timing when the water in the lower part of the steamer begins to simmer) and then turn into a dish and leave to cool.

Mix the vinegar with the olive oil and add the crushed garlic and tarragon leaves. Season with salt and pepper and mix well. Pour the marinade over the eggplant and mix again.

Cover with plastic wrap and leave to marinate in the refrigerator for at least 2 hours before serving.

Variation

You can replace the tarragon with other herbs. For example, try using mint in the marinade and sprinkle the eggplant with oregano before serving.

Bell peppers with garlic and basil

Serves 4

2 each red, yellow and orange bell peppers

olive oil

marinade

4 garlic cloves

1 bunch fresh basil

3/4 cup olive oil

salt and freshly ground black pepper

Rinse the peppers and blot dry with paper towels. Lightly coat with oil and then cut each into quarters lengthwise. Place the peppers, skin side up, under a preheated broiler—on a high setting, if the broiler is above the oven, or at an oven setting of 350°F if the broiler is in the roof of the oven—for about 20 minutes.

When the skins begin to blacken and blister, remove the peppers from the broiler and wrap in a plastic bag for about 30 minutes to loosen the skins.

While the peppers are under the broiler, peel and chop the garlic, and rinse and finely chop the basil leaves—leaving aside a few whole leaves for a garnish. Put the garlic and basil in a bowl, pour on the olive oil, season with salt and pepper, and mix well.

Peel the peppers, remove the seeds and cut into thin strips about 3/4 inch wide. Arrange in a shallow serving dish, alternating the colors, and pour over the marinade. Cover the dish with plastic wrap and leave to marinate in the refrigerator for at least 6 hours.

Remove the peppers from the refrigerator 1 hour before serving. Garnish with a few basil leaves.

Variation

Replace the garlic and basil with an onion sliced very thinly lengthwise, add a tomato, peeled and chopped, and 1 tablespoon of balsamic vinegar.

Mixed vegetable parcels

Serves 4

1 small eggplant

1 fennel bulb

1 red bell pepper

1 orange bell pepper

2 small zucchini

oil for cooking

marinade

6–8 shallots

1 garlic clove, peeled and grated

6 pieces sun-dried tomato, in oil

4 black olives, pitted and sliced

juice of 1 lemon

3 tablespoons olive oil

1 tablespoon flat-leaf parsley, chopped

1 teaspoon each fresh oregano and thyme

salt and freshly ground black pepper

The day before you want to serve the dish, cut the eggplant into 1/2-inch thick slices and place in a colander. Sprinkle with salt, cover with a weighted plate and leave to release their liquid for about 30 minutes. Rinse and blot dry with paper towels.

Clean the fennel, chop and plunge into a pan of boiling water, with a little added lemon juice, for 1 minute. Drain the fennel and place in a mixing bowl with the eggplant slices.

Rinse the bell peppers and zucchini, seed the peppers and cut into 1/2-inch strips. Cut the zucchini into 3/4-inch thick slices. Add to the eggplant and fennel.

To make the marinade, peel and finely chop the shallots. Heat a little oil in a pan and fry, over low heat, for 10 minutes. Add the garlic, stir for 20 seconds or so and remove from the heat. Stir in the sun-dried tomato and leave to cool.

Add the contents of the pan and the rest of the marinade ingredients to the bowl containing the vegetables and mix carefully. Cover with plastic wrap and leave to marinate in the refrigerator overnight, stirring the mixture just before you go to bed and again when you get up.

To prepare the parcels, preheat the oven to 400°F.

Divide the vegetable mixture between 4 pieces of waxed paper (about 12 inches square). Fold the sides of each piece of paper into the center and roll the ends to form a closed parcel (see picture opposite). Bake in the oven for 30 minutes. Serve immediately.

Zucchini with garlic and pink peppercorns

Serves 4

4 medium-sized zucchini

scant 1/2 cup olive oil

marinade

1 onion

5 garlic cloves

3/4 cup olive oil

1 teaspoon pink peppercorns

1 teaspoon oregano

salt and freshly ground black pepper

Rinse but don't peel the zucchini and cut each in half lengthwise. Coat each half with a little olive oil and place under a preheated broiler (see recipe on page 48), skin side up, for 15 minutes. Half way through cooking, turn them on their side without turning them over.

While the zucchini are cooking, peel and thinly slice the onion and garlic. Heat a scant 1/2 cup olive oil in a pan and lightly brown the onion over low heat for 2 minutes. Add the garlic and lightly brown with the onion for a further 2 minutes, taking care not to let the garlic burn.

Place the broiled zucchini, skin side down, in a shallow serving dish. Mix the onions and garlic with the pink peppercorns, oregano and the remaining olive oil. Pour the marinade over the zucchini, cover the dish with plastic wrap and leave to marinate in the refrigerator for at least 3 hours.

Remove the zucchini from the refrigerator around 1 hour before serving.

Fennel with pink grapefruit

Serves 4

2 fennel bulbs

3 pink grapefruit

marinade

6 tablespoons olive oil

juice of 1/2 lemon

juice of 1 grapefruit

1 teaspoon caraway (or cumin) seeds

salt and freshly ground black pepper

Trim the fennel stems but don't discard the feathery leaves. Clean the bulbs and slice thinly.

Peel one of the grapefruit and divide into segments, removing the membrane. Put into a shallow dish with the fennel.

Mix the olive oil with the lemon and grapefruit juice, add the caraway (or cumin) seeds and season with salt and pepper. Pour the marinade over the grapefruit segments and fennel.

Cover with plastic wrap and leave to marinate in the refrigerator for 3 hours, stirring from time to time.

Just before serving, peel the other 2 grapefruit, removing the membrane from each segment.

Remove the marinated fennel and grapefruit from the refrigerator, mix once more, and arrange the fresh grapefruit segments on the fennel. Garnish with chopped fennel leaves.

Fresh figs with mozzarella cheese

Serves 4

3 balls mozzarella (if possible use *mozzarella di bufala*—mozzarella made with buffalo's milk—as it has a more delicate flavor)

1 1/4 lb fresh figs, ripe and very sweet

3–4 fresh tarragon sprigs, leaves stripped

marinade

2 tablespoons walnut or hazelnut oil

2 tablespoons olive oil

juice of 1 lemon

1 garlic clove, peeled and chopped

salt and freshly ground black pepper

Drain the mozzarella and pat dry with paper towels. Cut into slices about 1/2 inch thick and arrange in a shallow dish.

To make the marinade, mix the 2 oils, lemon juice, and garlic. Season with salt and pepper and pour the marinade over the mozzarella. Cover with plastic wrap and leave to marinate in the refrigerator for at least 3 hours.

Just before serving, rinse and dry the figs and cut into slices about 1/2 inch thick. Arrange the slices of mozzarella on individual plates and top with the fig slices. Drizzle with the marinade and sprinkle with tarragon leaves.

Handy hint

If the figs are not very sweet, you can add a pinch of sugar to each slice.

Variation

For a stronger taste, use feta cheese instead of mozzarella.

Pears in spicy wine syrup

Serves 4

4 ripe pears

12 fresh mint leaves

marinade

2 cups red wine

1½ tablespoons blackcurrant liqueur

1 tablespoon brown cane sugar

3 cloves

1 cinnamon stick, broken in half

1 long vanilla bean, split in half lengthwise

rind of 1 unwaxed, or well-scrubbed, lemon, pared in thin strips with a zester

rind of 1 unwaxed, or well-scrubbed, orange, pared in thin strips with a zester

Put all the marinade ingredients in a pan and bring to a boil.

Peel the pears, cut them in half and remove the core. Add to the spiced wine and leave to simmer over low heat for 15 minutes, or until cooked through but firm—when they are cooked, you should be able to insert the blade of a knife into them easily. Do not let them overcook and become too soft.

Leave the pears to cool in the syrup and then transfer into a dish, cover and leave to marinate in the refrigerator for at least 1 hour.

Arrange the pears in individual dishes, drizzle with the syrup, and decorate with mint leaves.

Variation

You can use the whole orange and lemon by cutting them into segments (don't remove the peel) and simmering with the pears in the spicy wine. The syrup won't have any strips of rind in it, but guests who like citrus fruit will enjoy the orange and lemon segments with their peel intact but cooked.

Raspberries with fresh mint or lemonbalm

Serves 4

1 lb raspberries

marinade

2 cups water

½ cup Demerara sugar

1 long vanilla bean, split in half lengthwise

1 cinnamon stick, broken in half

a small handful of mint, or lemonbalm, leaves

juice of ½ lemon

Put the measured water and sugar into a pan with the vanilla bean and cinnamon, and bring to a boil. Boil for 5 minutes then remove from the heat and add the herb leaves. Cover and allow to infuse for 5 minutes, then remove the lid and leave to cool.

Transfer the syrup to a dish, cover, and chill in the refrigerator for 1 hour. Remove the vanilla bean, cinnamon stick, and herb leaves, and strain the syrup.

Return the syrup to the dish, add the raspberries, cover, and chill in the refrigerator for a further hour.

Just before serving, add the lemon juice and divide the raspberries and syrup between individual dishes. If the raspberries are not sweet enough, sprinkle with a little sugar.

Variation

Try this recipe with peaches and add a few raspberries just before serving.

Melon in spicy aniseed syrup

Serves 4

1 yellow flesh melon

1 orange flesh melon

marinade

1 pink grapefruit

½ cup cane-sugar syrup

1 long vanilla bean, cut in half lengthwise

1 cinnamon stick, broken in half

2 tablespoons aniseed-flavored liqueur (pastis, ouzo)

Squeeze the grapefruit and pour the juice into a pan. Add the cane-sugar syrup, vanilla bean, cinnamon stick, and aniseed liqueur, and bring to a boil. Reduce the heat and leave to simmer gently for 10 minutes. Remove from the heat and leave to cool.

Cut the melons in half and remove the seeds. Cut into thin slices and remove the skin.

Arrange the melon slices alternately in 4 individual dishes and pour on the cold syrup. Cover with plastic wrap and leave to marinate in the refrigerator for at least 3 hours.

Handy hint

You can save time by preparing the spicy grapefruit syrup the day before. It will keep overnight in the refrigerator.

Variation

For an even more refreshing dessert, replace the vanilla pod with grated ginger.

Tableware:

Manufacture de porcelaine Virebent

BHV (crockery)

Sentou galerie (cutlery and crockery)

Le Bon Marché (table mats)

Photographs: Akiko Ida

Styliing: Laura Zavan

This edition published by Hachette Illustrated UK, Octopus Publishing Group Ltd.,
2–4 Heron Quays, London E14 4JP

English translation by JMS Books LLP (email: Janem030@aol.com)

A CIP catalogue for this book is available from the Library of Congress

ISBN 10: 1 84430 156 7

ISBN 13: 978 1 84430 156 0

Printed by Toppan Printing Co., (HK) Ltd.